Dogs Wanna Have Fun

Volume 3

Emilie Bilokur

Good Life Collections

Published by Good Life Collections.

Dogs Wanna Have Fun Volume 3 / Emilie Bilokur.
1. Adult coloring books.   2. Dogs.   3. Pets.   4. Stress reduction.
ISBN-13: 978-0692648742

ISBN-10: 0692648747

DOGS WANNA HAVE FUN

Volume 3

Welcome to your Coloring Journey!

The wildly popular pastime of coloring is more important today than ever.

In these pages you will discover more than just a fun activity. You will find yourself reconnecting with your inner self – that deeper part of you that has been diminished by the stressful world we live in today.

Scientists have discovered important benefits that come from coloring. Spending time coloring reduces stress and eases worry. It also magically frees up that part of you that has gotten lost in the increasing chaos that has become our lives.

Use this book to unleash your creativity, and to nurture your inner self. Fill these pages with colors you love, and see how it makes you feel.

Where do you start? Trust your instincts. Let the colors and techniques take you where they will.

Color with passion and joy and abandon. Your inner self will love it.

And as always, have a magical journey.

My best coloring tips (and some things to help you experiment with color):

1. Place a piece of paper or card stock under the page you are coloring, just in case the color bleeds through. The card stock will also add a 'cushion'.

2. Cool colors such as blue, green and purple calm you down when you feel stressed. Use them to ease tension.
Warm colors such as red, orange and yellow lift a downhearted mood. Use them to feel cheerful.
Bright colors lift your spirits. Use them to feel carefree.
Pastels and light colors are soothing. Use them to take the hard edge off.
Dark colors soothe an overactive mind. Use them to wind down.

3. Shading will add depth to your design. After you have colored in an area with your colored pencil, go over parts of that same area again with the same pencil (or you can use a darker shade). Smooth over it with your white pencil to get a soft transition between the light and dark areas.

4. The training of many great artists has included studying the works done by great masters, and copying them. Don't be afraid to imitate color combinations, techniques and effects that you admire. You may be surprised that what you come up with is something that you like even better.

5. Forget rules. Do what you like and something unique will happen.

My favorite coloring tools:

Fiskars 48 Gel Pens (won't bleed through the page like many markers will)

Prismacolor Colored Pencils – thick lead and thin lead

Copic Ciao Art Markers – expensive but they color like a dream

Sakura Gelly Roll Gel Pens – a higher quality gel pen, expensive but delightful